R. H. (Robert Hindry) Mason

Norfolk photographically illustrated

R. H. (Robert Hindry) Mason

Norfolk photographically illustrated

ISBN/EAN: 9783742818720

Manufactured in Europe, USA, Canada, Australia, Japa

Cover: Foto ©Thomas Meinert / pixelio.de

Manufactured and distributed by brebook publishing software
(www.brebook.com)

R. H. (Robert Hindry) Mason

Norfolk photographically illustrated

NORFOLK

PHOTOGRAPHICALLY

ILLUSTRATED.

BY

R. H. MASON.

PHOTOGRAPHED AND PUBLISHED BY MASON AND CO.,

8, OLD BOND STREET, LONDON, AND 20, ST GILES STREET, NORWICH.

IN presenting this volume of Photographs to the Subscribers, I wish to record my obligations for the facilities I have received from most of the Nobility and Gentry in the County.

It has been well said, that "Great Britain may justly boast her decided superiority over every other State in Europe, in the grand display of its numerous Country Seats, presenting a succession of variety in the architectural embellishments, and surrounded by a landscape smiling with cultivation;" and it may be truly said that Norfolk occupies a proud position among English Counties in this respect. The magnificent Mansions here represented are a proof of the fact; and whilst Photography has faithfully represented their general appearance, I can but regret that it fails to convey any idea of the beautiful scenery by which these palatial residences of our County Families are surrounded. Many of them are also the depositories of most valuable collections of works of art and relics of antiquity.

It has been my desire to make this work as complete as possible, and I believe no place of importance has been omitted. There are some few Ruins in the County not here illustrated, but that arises from the fact that though in themselves they may possess a good deal of interest, yet they are so situated that no photograph could give an adequate idea either of their beauty or their extent. I may say of them generally, as Mr. White in his "Eastern England" says of Beeston Priory in particular, "The ruins are picturesque only in some of their accidents and details, not as a whole; here and there a buttress arrests your eye, or a sweep of mouldings, or the fragments of a cloister-like range, or the broken ivy-capped walls that environ an old tower and gaping east window."

The letterpress description of the several places, whilst it has no pretensions to originality, being chiefly compiled from sources well known and available to every one, will in all cases, I believe, be found correct, as I have spared no pains to secure accuracy in all the details.

R. H. M.

November, 1865.

CONTENTS.

NORFOLK

PHOTOGRAPHICALLY ILLUSTRATED.

NORWICH CATHEDRAL.

This, though neither the largest nor the finest of our cathedrals, and though its parts are of very different dates and styles, is a truly magnificent and imposing edifice. It consists of a nave and aisles, a transept, a choir, a chancel, with aisles continued round the semicircular east end, and four chapels. From the intersection of the choir and nave springs the tower and the spire. On the south side is a nearly perfect cloister. The entire length of the church is 411 feet, of the transepts 178 feet, the breadth of the nave and aisles is 72 feet, the height to the top of the tower is 140 feet, to the top of the spire 315 feet. When examined closely there is found much to admire in the exterior. The choir has a fine appearance; the light clerestory, with its rich perpendicular windows and bold flying buttresses, and semicircular termination rising out of the massive Norman base, has a very picturesque effect; as have also the Norman transepts. The tower is the most elaborate and loftiest of the Norman period remaining in England, and the spire is the loftiest in the kingdom, with the exception of that of Salisbury Cathedral, to which it must also yield in grace of proportions.

Of this cathedral we are enabled to trace the erection of all the principal proportions. The oldest part is as old as the see of Norwich. Herbert de Losinga, surnamed the Lay, on account of his flattering propensities, having been deposed from his bishopric of Thetford on account of some naughty doings, undertook a pilgrimage to Rome, in order to induce his Holiness to restore him to his office. He succeeded; and on his return, in 1094, Losinga, as he had obtained power to do, removed the see from Thetford to Norwich. For the site he purchased from the citizens a low piece of marshy ground, called the Cowholme. This tract he carefully drained; and, in 1096, laid the foundation of his cathedral, and close by that of a palace for himself, and a priory, which was to contain a principal and sixty monks. He lived to see a good part of the church erected, and died in 1119. It was completed by his successor, Eborard, who died in 1149, but had been deposed from his office four years previously. An old account, however, delays the completion of the cathedral till the time of John of Oxford, who died in 1200; but it is more probable that he only restored a part of it which had been injured by fire. Of this original church the choir, nave, aisles, transepts, and tower, with a couple of chapels attached, yet exist, though considerably altered by the insertion of more modern windows.

In 1272, on St. Peter and Paul's day, whilst the monks were at early service the cathedral steeple was violently struck by lightning, several large stones being thrown down, causing the worshippers to flee for fear, "the quire being full of stench and smoke."

In 1272 the cathedral, church, and monastery were set on fire by the citizens, in consequence of some disputes with the monks, and much injured. The citizens were excommunicated, and their liberties restrained. For this freak Edward I. sub-

sequently decreed that the citizens should pay 3,000 marks, in six years, to rebuild the church, by instalments of 500 marks a-year. That they should give to the use of the church a pix, or cup, weighing ten pounds in gold, worth a hundred pounds in money, to serve at the sacrament at the high altar in the cathedral.

The fabric being restored, on Advent Sunday, 1278, William de Middleton was enthroned Bishop of Norwich; and, on the same day the cathedral was consecrated in the presence of King Edward I. and Queen Eleanor, the Bishops of London, Hereford, and Waterford assisting, and there being present "many other earls, barons, and nobles."

Bishop Walpole, Richard de Uppenhall (a builder), Bishop Salmon, Henry de Well, John de Hancock, Bishop Wakering, Jeffery Synonds, and others, did much to extend and carry on the works. Bishop Walpole built a spire, which was blown down, whereupon the present one was built, about Jan., 1861. Under Bishop Percy's auspices the west end, with the great window, was built by Bishop Alnwych, about 1430.

In 1463 Bishop Lybert raised the splendid stone roof of the nave, repaved other parts of the cathedral, and erected a tomb over the founder, which was demolished during the great Rebellion.

In 1498 Bishop Goldwell built the roof of the choir, similar, but inferior work to the nave, adding the upper windows and flying buttresses.

In 1509, transepts injured by fire; repaired by Bishop Nix.

In 1601 the author of the Norwich Post tells us, "That on Wednesday, 29th April, a sudden storm of hail and rain fell, about 5 o'clock in the afternoon, which caused a great darkness, and a shock of thunder and lightning followed, with a noisome stink of brimstone, and in a moment the upper part of the spire of the cathedral was struck down, which, not long before, was finished, with the fane thereon. The stone and woodwork therein, for 20 feet in height, was cast down on the north roof of the church, which it brake down, shaked the walls and roof of the guiles and split the spire down the south part from top to bottom, sending about twenty holes that men might creep through on the north-west side; divers stones which fell out of them sunk above half a yard into the ground in the Bishop's garden; the damage of all parts of the roof about the steeple being estimated at £660. It was after evening service, else many had perished. William de Bourne, who, with Sir John Colter, was walking in the nave during the storm, saw that as the flash the whole church trembled, and the glass in the windows cracked; and, at a little hole in the west window, towards the north, fire entered, with a stink of brimstone, which, though small when it entered, grew large in the church, and smote down Colter to the ground, so that he had much ado to recover himself again; and that, though he was much terrified, he saw the fire go to the steeple the whole length of the church, and ascending thence, saw it no more, but feared to be killed by the fall of the church, the spire falling soon after upon the roof, as aforesaid; and the Rector of Thorpe, who had been at evening prayer, was sheltered in the gate-house, saw the lightning fall on a round ball of fire upon the church, and the spire and fane fell thereupon, and small a sulphurous stink. The fire in the steeple was extinguished, but was watched all night, and when the watchers went just gone, it brake out, about 4 o'clock in the morning, in a buttress of the cloister wall, and one of Dr. Suckling's servants narrowly escaped with his life; but it was soon extinguished. No other part of the city received any damage by this violent shock."

In 1861, January 16th, a "prodigious wind" from the south-west blew down the tower of the cathedral, and that beat down great part of the choir. The gale lasted six or seven days.

In 1845, the cathedral, though dedicated to the Holy Trinity, about this time began to be named Christ Church.

The Puritans treated the cathedral very badly. We learn from Sir Thomas Browne's *Repertorium*, that in stripping the cathedral to their service the Puritans, pretending to show their abhorrence of superstition, placed the seats of the Aldermen at the west end of the choir, and removed the pulpit, and altered the whole arrangement of the sittings of the congregation. At the Restoration the cathedral was, of course, in some measure, repaired, and a new organ was erected. Since then, it has been at different times repaired or restored in parts; but it still bears strong evidence of the disgraceful treatment it received.

The cathedral is situated so low, and is so much recconcealed by buildings, that it cannot be viewed as a whole from any near point; and the position chosen for our photograph is the exterior (the garden of the Bishop's palace) at present occupied by Canon Heaviside) is the only spot where a satisfactory view can be obtained without going a great distance, and so losing much of the beauty of the details of this glorious edifice.

ERPINGHAM GATE, NORWICH;

The north-west entrance from the city to the close. It bears the name of the Erpingham Gate from having been erected by Sir Thomas Erpingham, about the year 1400, at the instance, it has been said, of the warlike Bishop Spencer, to atone for the favour he had shown to the doctrines of Wickliffe. An interesting description of it is given by Blomefield; but what is there said of the word "Penn" being to be found in various places, and its bearing an air of penitence is most ingenious than well-founded. The word is "Yenk," equivalent to THINK, or BEWARE, which had is to be found as a motto to the crest of Sir T. Erpingham. His statue, in the attitude of praying, is still to be seen, in a state of good preservation, above. Sir Thomas has been described as "a good old countrimander and a most kind gentleman," to be mentioned by Shakespeare as leading his cloak to Henry V. on the eve of Agincourt; and as Froissart tells, had a chief share in winning that famous victory.

ST. ETHELBERT'S GATE, NORWICH.

This building, now the south-west entrance to the close, occupies a place originally filled by a parochial chapel, which, according to Blomefield, was, in its foundation, anterior to the Cathedral, but was burned down in the great conflicts of 1272. After the appeasing of the tumults, the citizens, in part of recompense for the injury done the convent, built the present gate, and over it a large handsome chapel, dedicated to St. Ethelbert; but, in process of time, the congregation falling off, it ceased to be applied to sacred purposes; and, even before the Reformation, was let for a private dwelling. It is at present used chiefly as a porter's lodge, this being the only place of egress or ingress to the close during the night.

ST. PETER'S MANCROFT CHURCH, NORWICH,

Is a large, regular, handsome building, and, next to the Cathedral, the leading ecclesiastical edifice in Norwich. It is well placed at the south-west corner of the market-place. According to Blomefield, it was finished and consecrated in the year 1455. It consists of a square tower at the west

end, 100 feet in height, and a body composed of a nave, choir, and chancel, measuring 212 feet in length by 70 feet in width. On the north and south side are entrance porches. The altar is ornamented with a painting representing the deliverance of St. Peter from prison. It was executed by Catton, and given to the church by Alderman Starling, in the year 1768. In the church, amongst other monuments, is one to the renowned Sir Thomas Browne, the learned doctor, whose *Urn Burial*, and other works, will long perpetuate his name and fame. The peal of bells in this church are very famous.

ST. NICHOLAS CHURCH, GREAT YARMOUTH.

Though so large a place, Yarmouth is but one parish, and, until 1714, had only this one church, which is one of the largest in the kingdom. It was originally built by Herbert de Losinga in 1123, and greatly enlarged in 1250 by Bishop Walter de Suthfield, and dedicated to St. Nicholas, the patron saint of fishermen. The transepts were added by Bishop Middleton, about 150 years after the original foundation. The building suffered much damage at the hands of the Puritans, and, during the Cromwellian period, the chancel was separated from the nave, one portion being used by Independents, and the other by another sect. The old spire was much injured by lightning in 1688, but it was not removed till the commencement of the present century, when, in 1806, the present one, 168 feet high, was substituted. The church has frequently undergone repairs, at considerable expense. So recently as 1848 nearly £6,000 were expended on the interior; and repairs amounting to a year or two since, and continue at this time, are estimated to cost £15,000 more. The nave of this church is 160 feet and the chancel 80 feet long, so that the extreme length of the fabric is 236 feet. The nave, or central aisle, is the narrowest, being only 30 feet wide, whilst the side aisles are each 39 feet wide. The transepts are 154 feet in length.

ST. MARGARET'S CHURCH, KING'S LYNN.

The chief architectural attractions of Lynn are its churches, of which it possesses several. The principal one is St. Margaret's, of which our photograph shows the west end. It was founded by Herbert de Losinga, Bishop of Norwich, in the reign of William Rufus. Its two towers are each eighty-six feet high; both stand upon the original Norman foundation, and the interior of the south-west tower has a rich display of Norman columns, arches, and arches of very early date. This tower has externally three stages of different styles of architecture, the lowest being transitional Norman, the second story early English, and the upper part Decorated. The buttresses at the angles are square, and very massive, and ended at the base of a series of lofty but slender clustered columns, with pointed arcades above. This tower is now embattled, and has crocketed pinnacles at the four corners, but was formerly surmounted by a spire, 298 feet high, which was blown down on the 8th September, 1741, destroying in its fall the nave, and also the lantern-tower, which rose from the four main arches at the intersection of the transepts with the nave and chancel. The north-west tower is all in the perpendicular style, and of four stages. It is terminated by a battlemented parapet, enriched with quatrefoil panels, and has eight crocketed pinnacles. There is a small porch over the western door, above which is a large seven-light window, of the perpendicular period, and to the gable is a niche containing a figure, now stated as St. Margaret. The length of this beautiful church is about 240 feet, and its width 130 feet. It is lighted by above seventy windows, nearly all of which were formerly filled with stained glass, and the roof is supported by twenty-two clustered columns, from which spring depressed arches. The interior contains much that is interesting, and, on the whole, it must be considered one of the finest churches in the kingdom.

WYMONDHAM CHURCH

Originally formed part of a monastery, founded 1130 by William de Albini. When the monastery was destroyed, the south aisle, over which were lodgings for supernumerary monks, was demolished. Anxious to save their noble church—erected in 1130,—a handsome cruciform building—the inhabitants obtained permission to use the abbey steeple, monks' lodgings over the south aisle, St. Margaret's Chapel, the chapel of the Virgin and St. Thomas à Becket, and the choir. However, the sacrilegious injustice of Mr. Serjeant Flowerdew defeated this intention, upon which the people took down the residuary buildings, and contented themselves with erecting the new aisle. The present church consists of a nave with aisles, a large western tower, and another at the intersection of the nave with the transepts. The ancient parts of the building display semicircular arches, with short columns and large piers, which appear to be part of the original structure. At the east end, and on the south side of the church, are some fragments of walls. The north aisle, porch, and tower, are of a much later date than the nave and south aisle; altogether, the church is an interesting and curious pile. It contains a large font, ornamented with bold sculpture, and elevated on steps.

BINHAM ABBEY.

All that is known of the origin of this building is, that Peter, Lord Valoines, nephew to the Conqueror, founded here a priory of Benedictine Monks, dedicated to St. Mary, as a cell to the Abbey of St. Alban's, but that it was not finished till the reign of Henry I. The interior, which is full of Norman arches, may probably be of the earliest of these eras. The west front, represented in the photograph, is evidently the work of the beginning of the thirteenth century; and, as is observed by Mr. Britton, in its arches, columns, mouldings, &c., nearly resembles the same features in the gable of Ely Cathedral, and in the western front and chapter-house of Salisbury Cathedral, all nearly of the same era. Though the priory is generally in ruins, the nave of the conventual church has been preserved, and still serves for the parish church. The font in it is highly ornamented.

CASTLE ACRE PRIORY.

Our photograph represents, probably, one of the finest and most perfectly preserved pieces of ruin in the kingdom, and though it is undoubtedly the best specimen of the remains of Castle Acre Priory, it by no means gives an idea of the extent of these ruins. This Priory was founded by the great Earl Warenne, in 1078, for monks of the Cluniac order.

NORTH CREAKE ABBEY.

In the year 1206 there was a church founded in a place called Lingerscroft, lying between Creake and Burnham. In the reign of Henry II. there was mass said in this church; but Sir Robert de Narford, being Constable of Dover Castle, under Hubert de Burgh, Chief Justice of England, and obtaining a victory over the French at sea, with the assistance of Alice, his wife, built a chapel to St. Bartholomew, with an hospital for thirteen poor lay brethren, four chaplains, and a master, or head. The walls of this abbey are shown in our general view; the choir is perfectly distinguishable, and the whole forms a fine, venerable ruin. The abbey estate is now held of Christ's College, Cambridgeshire, on a lease, renewable every seven years. The abbot and canons were of the order of St. Augustine.

WALSINGHAM ABBEY,

The most celebrated shrine in England in Roman Catholic times, was founded in 1061 by the widowed lady of Ricaldi Faverches, as a small chapel in honour of the Virgin Mary, similar to the Sancta Casa, at Nazareth. Sir Geoffrey, her son, confirmed the endowment, made an additional foundation of a priory for Augustine canons, and erected a conventual church. It was enriched by the piety of the superstition of succeeding generations, and at the dissolution, the annual revenues were valued, according to Speed, at £446 14s. 4d. The present remains of this once noble monastic pile, is a portal, or west entrance gateway, a richly ornamented lofty arch, sixty feet high, which formed the east end of the church, supposed to have been erected in the time of Henry

VII.; the refectory, seventy-eight feet long, and twenty-seven broad, and the walls twenty-six and a-half feet in height; a Saxon arch; part of the original chapel, which has a zig-zag moulding; part of the old cloisters; a stone bath, and two uncovered wells, called Wishing Wells. The view we have selected for illustration is the great arch, sixty feet in height, the remains of the east window of the ancient priory. The list of royal personages who came to this remote village includes Henry III., Edward I. and II., Henry VII. and VIII., David Bruce, King of Scotland (with twenty knights), and Queen Catherine.

THE ABBEY OF ST. BENNET AT HOLME

Consists only of a part of the old gate house. It was one of the twenty-nine mitred abbeys whose abbots, according to Tanner, statedly and constantly enjoyed the privilege of being called to Parliament. It is, moreover, remarkable, in conferring upon the Bishop of Norwich a title borne by no other person. On February 4th, 1535, Henry VIII., under the specious pretence of advancing the See, which in reality was greatly disparaged, severed the ancient barony and revenues from it, and annexed the Priory of Holme, and the barony and revenues of the Abbey of Holme, in lieu thereof. In right of this barony the Bishop of Norwich now sits in the House of Lords as Bishop of Holme; the barony of the bishopric being at present in the king's hand, and the monastery being never dissolved, only transferred by the statute. The Bishop of this See is the only Abbot at this day in England. Its foundation is traced so far back as the days of Canute, by whom, and Edward the Confessor, it was richly endowed. In Dugdale's Monasticon is given a plan of the church from a MS. in the Cottonian Library, which may afford some idea of the nature of the fabric. These ruins are in the parish of Horning, distant nine miles from Norwich.

CASTLE RISING CASTLE

Was erected by William de Albini, the first Earl of Essex, some time prior to the year 1176, on a hill to the south of Castle Rising. It was a noble pile, built on a similar plan to the Castle at Norwich. The square keep is in a hollow area, surrounded by a high bank and deep vallum. This bank was, however, formerly surmounted by a fortified wall, and its entrance formed by a bridge across the vallum and a lower gateway. To the east of these was an outer area, enclosed with a high bank and deep vallum, forming a sort of bastion to the citadel. The shell of the keep tower remains, with walls nine feet thick, and displays some ornamental windows, doorways, &c. The size of the great hall may still be ascertained. In this fortress, Isabel, Queen of Edward II., after the death of her favourite, Earl Mortimer, was confined from 1330 till her death in 1358. Here she was visited by her son, Edward III., accompanied, on one occasion, by his consort Philippa. The lordship of Rising afterwards fell to the Black Prince, and in the reign of Henry VIII. it became a possession of the Howards, who still retain it.

THE CASTLE, NORWICH,

Claims, according to some, a Danish origin. Blomefield imagines that the present structure was erected by Roger Bigod, in the time of William Rufus, and that it occupies the site of a brick building which was raised by Canute. In the reign of Henry II., it is stated by some writers, that Roger Bigod, who then possessed this fortress, materially altered the castle, and that the present keep tower is part of the work then erected. It occupied a considerable site of ground. Blomefield says, " The extent of the outermost ditch reached on the west part to the edge of the present market-place; on the north to London Lane, which it included; and on the east almost to Conisford Street. The postern, or back entrance, was on the north-east part for a communication to the site of the Earl's Palace, the precinct of which adjoined and contained the whole space between the outward ditch and Tombland. The southern part reached to the Golden Ball

Lane. where the grand gate stood.' Over each foss was a bridge; one of them which remains, Mr. Wilkin says, " is the largest and most perfect arch of Saxon workmanship in the whole kingdom." At the inner extremity of it are the foundations of two circular towers, of 14 feet in diameter, one of which was appropriated to condemned criminals till 1793, when the new buildings were erected. Near the south-west angle of the inner vallum is the square keep tower, the antiquity and architecture of which have afforded a very fertile theme for disputation. The interior of the keep is now an unroofed area, but was formerly divided by floors, covered in at the top, and separated into several spacious apartments. The basement floor appears to have been vaulted over with stone, some vestiges of which are still to be traced. It is conjectured that the well was situated in the middle of the keep. Within this fortress there was formerly a royal chapel, exempt from all episcopal jurisdiction. In the year 1793 a new gaol was erected for the county, and it was resolved to build it on the Castle Hill, and attach it to the eastern side of the old edifice. Sir John Soane, the architect, was officially engaged, and the building was completed from his designs. The Castle Precinct contains 6 acres, 1 rood, and 13 perches, and the summit of the hill is in circumference 360 yards. The whole of the latter is enclosed with iron palisades and iron gate. Under an Act of Parliament, passed in 1806, the Castle and its limits are vested in the Justices of the Peace for the County, in trust, by which they are empowered to rebuild, repair, or alter any part belonging to it, as they may think proper.

ST ANDREW'S HALL

This noble fabric was formerly the conventual church of the Benedictine Monastery of Blackfriars. Blomefield says it was begun in 1415 by Sir Thomas Erpingham, Knight, and finished by his son, Sir Robert, who was Rector of Bracon, and one of the fraternity. But other authorities have placed the date subsequent to 1450. It consists of a nave and two aisles, which remain nearly perfect. Formerly it had a handsome steeple, which stood in the centre between the nave and the choir, but it was neglected, and fell down in 1712. The aisles are separated from the nave by six elegantly proportioned columns, which support the roof. They are half the breadth of the nave, and of the same length. The whole is about 120 feet long and 70 feet wide within the walls. There are fourteen windows on a side in the upper tier and six in the lower, two at the east, and three at the west. These were formerly ornamented with painted glass. Ultimately, the Hall passed into the hands of the Corporation; but before then it had been the domicile of the Guild of St. George the Martyr. Queen Elizabeth, and King Charles II. and his Queen, have here been feasted and honoured. In the hall are more than fifty pictures of interest and value. At the east end is a full-length portrait of Queen Anne, and another of her Consort, Prince George of Denmark. There is also an admirable portrait of Nelson, with this inscription, "The best likeness of this illustrious hero, and the last for which he ever sat, was painted after his return from the Battle of the Nile, in the year 1801, by Sir William Beechey, and confers additional lustre on the professional abilities of that artist." There are also portraits of Robert, Earl of Oxford, Horace Walpole, Lord Hobart, &c. It is in this noble hall the triennial musical festivals are held, and the Church Congress of 1865 was held here. But it is often used for very ignoble purposes.

BISHOP'S BRIDGE, NORWICH,

Says Blomefield, was so called because it led directly to the Bishop's palace, and in 1249 belonged to the see, it being then repaired by the priors of Norwich and St. Leonard; but afterwards, being a general inlet into the city, it was resolved to place it in the citizens' hands, and accordingly it has belonged to and been maintained by the city ever since 1393, and they always appointed a porter to live near and keep the gates; but the hermit, which dwelt by them, was always nominated by the prior, and the hermit's house at the dissolution was assigned to the church.

THE NELSON MONUMENT AT YARMOUTH

Stands on the South Danes, about a mile from the town, and was erected from a design by Mr. William Wilkins, an architect. The first stone was laid by the Hon. Colonel Wodehouse, on the 15th of August, 1817, and the column is 144 feet in height. Upon the plinth are the names of the four flag-ships on board which Nelson commanded at the battles of Aboukir, St. Vincent, Copenhagen, and Trafalgar; and the names of these victories are inscribed on the coping of the terrace. The roof is surmounted by caryatides, surmounted by a statue of Britannia holding a trident in one hand and a wreath of laurel in the other. The following inscription appears on the west side of the monument :—

HORATIO, LORD NELSON,
Whom, as her first and proudest champion in naval fight,
Britain honoured, while living, with her favour,
and when lost, with her tears;
Of whom, signalised by his triumphs in all lands,
the whole earth
stood in awe on account of the tempered fierness of
his counsels, and the undeauded ardour of his courage;
This great man,
NORFOLK
boasts her own, not only as born there of a
respectable family, and as there having received his
early education, but her own also in talents,
manners and mind.
The glory of so great a name, though sure long to
outlive all monuments of brass and stone,
his fellow-countrymen of Norfolk have resolved to commemorate
by this column, erected by their joint contributions.
He was born in the year 1788;
Entered on his profession in 1771;
and was concerned in nearly 120 naval
engagements with the enemy;
Being conqueror, among various other occasions,
At Aboukir, August, 1798;
At Copenhagen, April, 1801;
And at Trafalgar, October, 1805;
Which last victory, the crown of so many glorious achievements,
he consecrated by a death, equally mournful to his
country and honourable to himself.

THE COKE MONUMENT AT HOLKHAM.

This column, 120 feet in height, was commenced in 1845, and has on the four corners of its pedestal a Devon ox, a Southdown sheep, a plough, and a drill; whilst on three sides of the pedestal are bas-reliefs representing Mr. Coke granting a lease to a tenant, the Holkham sheep-shearing, and irrigation; and on the fourth side the following inscription :—

This column, in memory of
THOMAS WILLIAM COKE, EARL OF LEICESTER,
For more than half a century
the faithful Representative of this County
in the House of Commons,
erected by tenantry
originating with the Tenantry, and supported by the
Noblemen and Gentlemen of all parties,
Records a life devoted to the welfare of his Friends,
Neighbours and Tenants,
Of such a man
Contemporaries needed no memorial; his Deeds
were before them; his fortune in their hearts;
But it repays Posterity to know that by pre-eminently
combined Public Services with Private Worth;
affording an illustrious example of birth and station,
refunded by Duty and inspired by Benevolence,
Integrity and Independence, united for public and private;
Near Monster and Regret
blessed the Father, Friend, and Landlord.
The Arts lament to him a liberal and fostering Patron;
and Agriculture, to which
from early manhood to the close of life, he dedicated
Time, Energy, Science, and Wealth,
Crowning his Greatness with her successes,
cherishes the proudest and commands the gratitude
of her great Promoter and Benefactor.

THE TOWN HALL, LYNN,

Or Trinity Hall, is an ancient building of stone and flint. It consists of apartments, the first of which is the stone hall, in which the County Quarter Sessions and Town Sessions are held. This hall is 53 feet long and 27 feet wide, and proportionately lofty. It contains the portraits of Sir Robert Walpole, full length; Sir Thomas White, the liberal benefactor to young tradesmen, half length; Sir Benjamin Keen; George II., a full length; and Lord Nelson. In 1808, portraits of Edward VI. and James I. were presented to this hall by Ald. Robinson.

GREY FRIARS TOWER, LYNN.

The Grey Friars, Friars Minn, or Franciscans' Convent, was founded about 1264 by Thomas Feltham. It was built in Fuller's Row, near St. James's Street, near the present Mill Lane. The remains of this building, a hexagon tower, with pointed windows, which is well represented in our photograph, serves as a good landmark to vessels entering the harbour.

AN ANCIENT DOORWAY AT ARMINGHALL.

The only account left us of the building to which this beautiful porch belongs, is derived from Blomefield; and states no more than that it was erected by Nicholas, son of Nicholas Hawe, of Trowthan, who settled here, and who was clerk to the Crown. This would bring the date to about 1000, but Colman is not satisfied with placing it so late. "The pointed arch, and en-circled admits the not at all correspond with the architecture, and particularly the domestic architecture, then in use. I am rather, therefore, led to suppose the porch a relic of one of the dissolved religious houses, or, perhaps, of one which endeavoured again to raise its head in the days of Mary. From its being made of wood, and from the general character of its ornaments (the latter I think most probable), I would date it about 1055. The supposition of its having belonged to some monastery, is still further strengthened by a tradition which I have since understood to exist, that it was brought from the ruins of Carrow Abbey, by which it is believed that various parts of the surrounding country were enriched." As tending to illustrate the sculpture of the times, this porch is a particularly valuable relic. The figures over the inner door, which is richly carved, appear to have relation to some legendary tale, and have, probably on that account, been so mutilated as to be no longer distinguishable. The doorway under the porch is perpendicular, with the original oak door, having carved upon it, "Pray for the soul of William Elr, 1487." Over the north door is a coat of arms, and round it runs a beautiful wreath of vine-leaves. The house is occupied by a farmer.

ASHWELLTHORPE HALL,

Situated about nine miles from Norwich, is the property of Lord Berners. The view given in this work represents the modern part of the hall, built in 1831, on the site of the old hall, which had a moat and drawbridge, and of which a small part still remains. Further additions were made in 1845.

BARNINGHAM HALL,
The Seat of John Thomas Mott, Esq.,

Is eight miles from Cromer, and situated in the parish of Barningham-Winter, so called from the family of the Winters, who held this lordship in the reign of Edward III. In 1385, and again in 1390, (the 4th and 16th of Richard II.) William Winter of Barningham-Winter, Armiger, was sheriff of Norfolk and Suffolk. In the latter part of the reign of Elizabeth, it was possessed by the Pastons, and the older house, which stood on a lower site, being pulled down, Sir Edward Paston, Knight, in 1612, built the present mansion, as appears by the arms of Paston impaling Berney, in a shield over the entrance-porch, with this date; Sir Edward having married for his second wife Margaret, daughter of Henry Berney, Esq., of Reedham. About the year 1756, Thomas Paston, Esq., fifth in descent from the above, sold the property to William Russell, a London merchant, from whom it passed into the hands of Thomas Lane, Esq., and he, in 1772, sold it to Thomas Vertue Mott, Esq., grandfather of the present owner. The house was much enlarged, and the south or garden front altered, in 1807, under the direction of Mr. Humphrey Repton, architect, but the west, or entrance front, a fine example of the time of James I., remains in its original state, in which the lofty double dormer is a peculiar feature.

EAST BARSHAM HALL.

This fine old Manor-house, situated three miles from Fakenham, is the property of Lord Hastings, and is one of the most interesting specimens remaining of the domestic architecture of the reign of Henry VII. It was built by Sir William Fermor in 1536, and afterwards became the seat of the Calthorpes. It is ornamented with moulded brick, in bands of panels charged with various shields and heads, ogee canopies with crockets and finials, hollow mouldings filled with roses, octagonal and round turrets, and handsome chimnies, enriched with fleur-de-lis and roses. Over the gateway are the royal arms, supported by the greyhound and the griffin, with the portcullis in the corners.

BAWDESWELL HALL

Is on the turnpike road from Norwich to Fakenham, and occupied by Clarke Stoughton, Esq. It is a red brick mansion, of Elizabethan architecture, built in 1633, and has been recently restored.

BLICKLING HALL,
The Seat of the Most Hon. the Marquis of Lothian.

Before the Norman Conquest this manor was held by Harold (for a short time king; but at the Doomsday survey, it was held in two moieties—one by the Crown, and the other by the Bishop of Thetford. The Conqueror settled the whole on the one; and after the foundation of Norwich Cathedral, the bishop of the diocese has been a palace or country seat. In 1431, Blickling became the property of Sir Thomas Erpingham, who sold it to Sir John Fastolf, of whom it was purchased in 1452, by Sir Geoffrey Boleyne, who was Lord Mayor of London in 1457. It next passed to Sir Thomas Boleyn, father of the unfortunate Anne Boleyn and Viscount Rochford, both of whom were born here and who were beheaded in the reign of Henry VIII. From the Boleyns the manor passed to the family of Cleves, one of whom sold it to Sir Henry Hobart, Lord Chief Justice of the Common Pleas. His son, Sir John, himself in 1920, which marks the third time. One of his descendants, John Hobart, was created Earl of Buckinghamshire in 1746. On the death of the second Earl of Buckinghamshire, without male issue, in 1793, this estate passed to his second daughter, Lady Caroline Hobart, who married the second Lord Suffield, and died without issue in 1850, when she was succeeded by her grandnephew, the present Marquis of Lothian. Blickling Hall is almost hid a little more than a mile from Aylsham, and its ground-plan is quadrangular, with two open courts in the centre. At each angle of the edifice is a square turret, terminated by a vane, while over the entrance is a clock-tower of more modern character. The entrance from the court in front formed by the stables and offices is over a bridge, with two arches, that spans a moat. Upon the ancient hall-door is the date "Anno Dni 1620." In the upper story of this noble mansion is a large window, with twelve compartments formed by stone mullions. The hall, which leads to the anterchamber, is forty-two feet long, thirty-three feet wide, and the same in height. It opens on the great staircase, which branches off to the right and left, conducting to a grand gallery of communication. In this are full-length pictures of Anne Boleyn and Queen Elizabeth. In the library are 10,000 volumes. Blickling has been twice visited by royalty. In 1671, King Charles and his Queen were there. Stevenson has thus attempted to treat the subject poetically:

"Blickling, for mansions, and like queens for mode, One long blushed dames, another breath'd a queen."

BOYLAND HALL,
The Seat of Frederick William Irby, Esq.,

Is in the parish of Morningthorpe, eleven miles from Norwich, and was formerly a moated house, having a drawbridge, &c. As the photograph shews, it is a handsome Elizabethan mansion. It was built in 1571, and was thoroughly repaired and restored in 1804 by Admiral the Hon. F. P. Irby, who collected on the coast of Africa a large quantity of coarse shells, with which he studded the interior of an alcove, in a shrubbery adjacent to the hall, which had over the entrance porch a fine bust of Queen Elizabeth, removed from a niche at the demolition of Tilbury House. There are a number of very valuable royal portraits preserved in this hall.

BUCKENHAM-TOFTS HALL,

The Seat of the Right Hon. LORD ASHBURTON,

Is distant from Thetford eight miles, and is a conveniently-arranged mansion, originally founded, in the reign of Charles the Second, by a Mr. Vincent.

BURLINGHAM HALL,

The Seat of HENRY NEGUS BURROUGHES, ESQ.,

As the photograph shows, is a plain modern mansion, situated about eight miles from Norwich, and has no pretension to architectural merits. It is the seat of a family that has long been influential in the county, and the present occupier represented the Eastern Division of Norfolk in Parliament for several years.

BYLAUGH HALL,

The Seat of the Rev. HENRY EVANS LOMBE,

Is a fine modern mansion, built of stone, and well represented in our view from the garden terrace. It is distant six miles from East Dereham.

COSSEY HALL,

The Seat of the Right Hon. LORD STAFFORD,

Is situated about five miles and a-half from Norwich. The old hall, which is chiefly shown in one of our views of this magnificent building, is in the plain Tudor style, with battlements and square windows. It forms three sides of a quadrangle, and the projecting wings are terminated by corbiestepped gables, crowned by square pinnacles. This house was erected by Sir Henry Jerningham in the reign of Elizabeth, and will be removed when the new and splendid mansion (commenced upwards of thirty years ago) is completed. The manor of Cossey, or Costessey, was given by the Conqueror to Alan, Earl of Richmond. After passing from him through various families, it was granted by Queen Mary to her Vice-Chamberlain, Sir Henry Jerningham, mentioned above. The family of Jernegam, or Jeruingham, was famous even before the Conquest, one of its members having obtained several manors in Norfolk from Canute, as a reward for the services he had rendered to Sweyne, King of Denmark, when he invaded England. Henry Jerningham was created a baronet in 1621. His descendant, the late Sir George Jerningham, was heir-general of the bodies of Sir William Howard and Mary Stafford, his wife. This Sir William Howard was created Baron Stafford, after espousing the heiress of the Stafford family, in 1640; but being iniquitously attainted as a conspirator in the Popish plots, he was beheaded in 1678. By the reversal of this unjust attainder in 1825, the father of the present Lord Stafford succeeded to the title. Among the pictures in this hall is a portrait of Queen Mary, by Holbein, and a very curious drawing by Philip Fruytius, dated 1640, representing the Earl of Arundel, his countess, Alethea, and three children. There are also portraits of James II. and his family. Close to the house is a modern chapel, built under the direction of Edward Jerningham, Esq., in the Gothic style. It has lofty windows, with pointed arches, mullions, &c., each of which is filled with stained glass, of great value, collected from various continental monasteries. The whole produces a beautiful effect.

CRANMER HALL,

The Seat of SIR WILLOUGHBY JONES, BART.,

Was built in the early part of the eighteenth century. The estate was purchased by Mr. Jones in 1751, and has since continued in the present family. The Jones' of Cranmer were originally a Welsh family, from Carmarthenshire. Sir John Jones, who was created a baronet for his military services, was a distinguished engineer officer, who received a gold medal for the capture of Badajos, which has since been borne by the family in their coat of arms. The present baronet, who is now engaged in making considerable improvements in the Hall, especially in beautifying its interior, was High Sheriff of the county in 1851, and has been Chairman of the County Sessions since 1856. Cranmer Hall is situated in the parish of Sculthorpe, distant about two miles from Fakenham.

CROMER HALL,

The Seat of BENJAMIN BOND CABBELL, ESQ.

This Hall formerly belonged to the Windham family, but some time since became the property of Mr. Cabbell, who occasionally resides here. It is situated nearly a mile from the town of Cromer, on the road to Felbrigg; and from the grounds of the house beautiful views are obtained of the surrounding scenery and of the German Ocean.

ELMHAM HALL,

The Seat of the Right Hon. LORD SONDES,

Is situated a few miles from East Dereham, and, as the photograph shows, is a large family mansion, designed rather with a view to domestic convenience than architectural pretensions. It was built about the year 1725, by Richard Warner, Esq., and since its possession by Lord Sondes has received considerable additions.

ELSING HALL

Is an ancient moated mansion, at present occupied by Richard Charles Browne, Esq., who is Lord of the Manor. It was the property of the Folicts, until Sir Richard Foliot's daughter Margery married Sir Hugh Hastings, commander of the army of Edward III. in Flanders; and it was the residence of the Hastings family, until it passed, by the marriage of Anne, eldest daughter and co-heiress of Sir Hugh Hastings, to William Browne, shortly before the year 1554. The hall appears to have been originally erected in the thirteenth century, as the foundations and some fragments built into the walls, are believed to be of that date; but it was probably rebuilt, or considerably altered, about 1550. During the last two centuries, it has suffered much from alterations and destruction, though it still retains some features of considerable interest.

FELBRIGG HALL,

Three miles from Cromer,—the seat formerly of the Windham family—stands at the eastern extremity of a high tract of land, called Felbrigg and Sherrington Heaths, and is generally considered to be one of the finest situations in the whole county. It is an Elizabethan structure, which has been much enlarged at different times, and is now not only commodious, but elegant. This fine estate was recently sold to Mr. Kitton, a merchant, of Norwich.

GUNTON HALL,

The Seat of the RIGHT HON. LORD SUFFIELD.

This Hall, which has long been the seat of the Harbord family, was much enlarged, under the direction of Mr. Wyatt, in 1785, and now presents an extensive range of commodious apartments. The hall is situated about five miles from Cromer, and an equal distance from Aylsham.

HAVERLAND HALL,

The Seat of EDWARD FELLOWES, ESQ., M.P.,

Is situated nine miles from Norwich. It is a fine specimen of Italian architecture, from designs by Mr. Blose, and was built by Mr. Fellowes in 1842.

HEYDON HALL,

The Seat of W. E. L. BULWER, ESQ.,

Is six miles from Aylsham. The house is an Elizabethan structure, built in 1584, and is situated upon an elevated table-land, from which circumstance it has evidently derived its mrus—high down corrupted into Heydon. It was formerly possessed by the Earles, having been purchased by the distinguished lawyer, Erasmus Earle, own Serjeant-at-Law to Oliver Cromwell. By the marriage of the eminent lawyer's descendant with William Bulwer, Esq., of Wood Dalling, and Guestwick, Heydon came to the family of the Bulwers, who have held lands, and resided at Wood Dalling since the Conquest. The eldest son of this marriage with the heiress of Heydon, was William Earle Bulwer, Esq., a Brigadier-General in the army, and Colonel of the 106th Foot; who married Elizabeth, daughter of Richard Warburton Lytton, Esq., of Knebworth Park, Herts, and died in 1807, leaving three sons, William Earle Lytton Bulwer, Esq., now of Heydon Hall; Sir Henry Lytton Bulwer, K.C.B.; and the distinguished novelist and statesman, Sir Edward Lytton Bulwer Lytton, Bart., of Knebworth.

HILLINGTON HALL,

The Seat of SIR W. HOVELL BROWN FFOLKES, BART.,

Situated about seven miles from Lynn, was built in 1627 by Richard Hovell, upon a manor belonging to the Abbot of Dereham. In 1693, Sir William Hovell dying without male issue, this estate devolved to one of his daughters, who married Martin Ffolkes, Esq., an ancestor of the present owner. Within the last few years the hall has been much improved. It now presents a handsome elevation, in the Gothic style.

HOLKHAM HALL,

The Seat of the Right Hon. the EARL OF LEICESTER.

The manor of Holkham was held by the Balyers till 1504, when it passed to Lady Ann Gresham. A capital messuage at Holkham Staith, with lands in Holkham, were for many generations held by the ancestors of one Edmund Newgate, who in 1862 sold all his property to John Coke, Esq., fourth son of Lord Chief Justice Sir Edward Coke, who had previously purchased the manor and all the other land in the parish. His successor, Thomas Coke, was, in 1728, created Baron Lovel, of Minster-Lovel, Oxfordshire, and in 1744, Viscount Coke, of Holkham, and Earl of Leicester; but dying without issue in 1760, his titles became extinct. This Earl it was who converted the barren heath of Holkham into a beautiful estate. He commenced the erection of the present hall (or House, as it is sometimes called), in 1734, and it was finished by his widow in 1760. This mansion may be said to consist of five quadrangles; that is, of a large central building and four wings, so that each side presents a regular and perfect front. With some trifling variations, this resembles Palladio's plan of a villa, designed for the Cavalier Leonardo Moceniga, upon the Brenta. The extent, including the wings, is 344 feet by 180 in depth. In the house is a splendid collection of pictures. The names of some of the leading artists will alone suffice to give the connoisseur an idea of want is to be seen at Holkham. Lanfranc, Guido, Titian, Carlo Maratti, Rubens, Anibal Caracci, Vandyke, Sebastian Concha, Canaletti, Gaspar Poussin, Raphael, Parmegianus, Paul Veronese, Leonardo da Vinci, Claude Loraine, &c., besides some antiques and choice pieces of sculpture. Holkham also has a fine library, and a valuable collection of MSS. The late Mr. Coke, who, after representing the county in parliament for fifty-seven years, was created (in 1837) Earl of Leicester and Viscount Coke, was the son of Wenman Roberts, Esq., who assumed the name of Coke on succeeding to the estates of his maternal uncle, Thomas Coke, Earl of Leicester, mentioned above. Holkham Hall is distant from Wells two miles, and is thirty-two miles from Norwich.

HONINGHAM HALL,

The Seat of the REV. LORD BAYNING,

Was built in the reign of Queen Elizabeth, by Lord Chief Justice Richardson, with the exception of the more modern south front. It is situated seven miles from Norwich.

HOUGHTON HALL,

The Seat of the Most Hon, the MARQUIS OF CHOLMONDELEY,

Is a truly sumptuous pile, intimately connected with the fame and fortune of Sir Robert Walpole. The original designs were furnished by Colin Campbell, author of "Vitruvius Britannicus;" but the mansion was erected by Thomas Ripley. It was commenced in 1722, and finished in 1735. The principal front is toward the west. The main building is quadrangular, and 166 feet square. The basement story is rustic; this is ascended by a double flight of steps, with a balustrade. The pediment over the entrance is supported by Ionic columns. The wings, containing the offices, are connected with the main body of the edifice, by a Tuscan colonnade, and the extent of the whole front is 450 feet. The interior contains a suite of magnificent apartments, adorned in the most sumptuous manner. The great hall, a cube of forty feet, is certainly a very noble room. The drawing-room is thirty feet long by twenty-one feet wide. In the library, is a whole length portrait of George I., in his coronation robes, by Sir Godfrey Kneller; this is the only picture for which that monarch ever sat in England. Paintings and sculpture of great value adorn more or less the apartments. Though thought its chief boast, its large and celebrated collection of pictures was sold in 1779, by George, Earl of Orford, to Catherine, Empress of Russia, for £45,500, a sum far below their real value. Houghton is thirteen miles from Lynn, and ten miles from Fakenham.

HUNSTANTON HALL

Has for many ages been the seat of the distinguished family of Le Strange, it having originally come into their possession by the marriage of Roland Le Strange, in the eleventh century, to the sole heiress of the original Saxon possessors of the manor. The most ancient portion of Hunstanton Hall now remaining is the north-west angle, which dates back to the reign of Edward IV. The gateway was erected by Sir Roger Le Strange, who died in 1509, and who was "Esquire of the body" to Henry VII. It was originally quite distinct from the rest of the edifice; but in 1623, Sir Hamon Le Strange added the two wings, together with the north and south sides of the inner quadrangle, and thus united it with the inhabited part of the hall. He also built the embattled wall round the outer court, as well as the gateway to it, and the doorkeeper's lodge in the park. The hall was well restored in 1830; but a fire having broke out in 1853, entirely destroyed most of the principal rooms, among others, the ancient baronial dining-hall. This hall is situated about seventeen miles from Lynn.

INGLETHORPE HALL, EMNETH,

The Residence of CHARLES METCALFE, ESQ.,

Is a modern structure, erected by the present proprietor in the year 1857, and is a good specimen of the adaptation of the Tudor style of architecture to the requirements of modern conveniences. It is constructed of a richly-coloured red brick, and the ornamental moulded brickwork may bear comparison with the old manor-houses of early date. The ancient manor of Bellasis, or Ingoldsthorpe's Manor (variously written Inglethorpe,) as well as the manor of Hagbech, in Emneth, came into the possession of the present family in the year 1805, by purchase from Sir Henry Peyton, Bart., whose ancestor, Sir Thomas, purchased both manors, with other estates, from Hewar Oxburgh, Esq., in 1720. Hagbech Hall, a residence of the Peytons for eighty-five years, and the original manor-house of Hagbech, was taken down in the year 1808. The land surrounding Inglethorpe Hall was formerly a race-ground, and being, in the year 1857, allotted on the inclosure of the commons as the manorial allotment, it has been appropriately selected as a site for the manor-house of both manors.

KETTERINGHAM HALL,

The Seat of SIR JOHN PETER BOILEAU, BART.

At the time of the Conquest, the Ketteringham estates, now held by Sir John Boileau, passed to Roger Bigod and Randulph Fururell, and from them to the Vaux, Vere, and other families.

In 1261, the manor came by marriage to the Argentines; and it afterwards became the property of the Grey, Heveningham, Heron, Atkyns, and Peach families. In 1886, Ketteringham was conveyed to John Peter Boileau, Esq., of Tacolnestone Hall, who, in 1838, on the coronation of Queen Victoria, was created a baronet. The Hall, the front of which is shown in our photograph, is a handsome castellated Tudor mansion, of ancient foundation, has been considerably enlarged and improved by its present owner, especially by the erection of the spacious Gothic banqueting-hall. The house is richly stored with paintings, books, and choice monuments of antiquity, including a fine collection of arms and armour: it is situated about seven miles from Norwich.

KIMBERLEY HOUSE,
The Seat of the RIGHT HON. LORD WODEHOUSE.

This estate was formerly the property of the family of Pateshull, when the hall stood on the west side of the village of Kimberley. In the reign of Henry IV., it was pulled down by Sir John Wodehouse, who had married the heiress of Sir John Pateshull, and a noble mansion, called Wodehouse Tower, was erected, where the family resided till the middle of the seventeenth century, when it was pulled down. The present seat was erected by Sir John Wodehouse, 1712, and four towers (one at each angle), were added by Sir Armine Wodehouse, who also made several other improvements. The house, which is built of brick, contains many convenient rooms, a spacious library, and others detached. The park is a fine one, richly ornamented with wood and water, and stocked with deer. In the house is preserved a fine portrait of Vandyck, painted by himself when young, also a seal ring, given by Catherine, Queen of Henry V., to the wife of John Wodehouse, who was esquire of the body to Henry V., and who distinguished himself at Agincourt. Queen Elizabeth lodged here in 1578, on her journey from Norwich to Cambridge, and part of the dress which she wore on that occasion is still in the possession of the family. Kimberley House is situated about four miles from Wymondham.

LANGLEY HALL,
The Seat of SIR THOMAS WILLIAM BROGRAVE PROCTOR BEAUCHAMP, BART.,

Is near the small town of Loddon. The date of this house is uncertain. It was bequeathed with a considerable estate, by George Proctor, Esq., in 1744, to his nephew, Sir William Beauchamp, the first baronet, who added the name and arms of his uncle to his own. Sir William Beauchamp Proctor, was a Knight of the Bath. He represented the County of Middlesex in Parliament from 1747 to 1768, having successfully contested the seat on various occasions with the celebrated Wilkes, for which he was honoured with the friendship of the king, George III., who presented him with his portrait, which is amongst the numerous pictures in the hall. Langley Hall is a magnificent structure, but it is difficult to say to what style of architecture it exactly belongs. Perhaps the term Anglo-Italian may be most appropriate. The centre, or main building, is in five divisions, with a portico of Doric order; but the two original wings have been pulled down and rebuilt. Few English seats are richer than Langley Hall in works of art, of the very highest order. We have only to name Michael Angelo, Salvator Rosa, Nicolas Bergem, Canaletti, Vandervelde, Andre del Sarto, Wouvermann, Teniers, Vandyck, Leonardo da Vinci, Claude, Albert Durer, the two Poussins, Murillo, Cornelius Jansen, besides numerous antiques, marbles, rare china, and many paintings of the best English masters, such as Gainsborough, Wilson, and Sir Joshua Reynolds.

LOVELL'S HALL, KING'S LYNN,
The Seat of the Rev. THOMAS THOROGOOD UPWOOD,

Is situated in the parish of Terrington St. Clement, and is distant four miles from Lynn. It is believed to have been of very considerable extent, and to have been built in 1543. It has been inhabited by the Upwood family for many generations. One of the apartments contains a large piece of beautiful Gobelin tapestry, representing, in all the richness of a painting, a numerous group of figures from Orlando Furioso, some of them as large as life.

ST. MARY'S HALL, KING'S LYNN,
The Seat of GUSTAVUS HELSHAM, ESQ.,

Is situated in the parish of Wiggenhall St. Mary the Virgin, about four miles from King's Lynn. The present residence has been erected at different periods, the centre having been originally the embattled gatehouse of a more ancient hall or manor-house, which was a very extensive brick building, erected, no doubt, by the family of Kervile, or Capervill, whose arms, with those of the Plowdens', were to be found thereon. The name of the parish is said to date from the thirteenth century, when one "Wiggenhale," a follower of the Conqueror, became owner of the estate of which the parish formed a part. The Kerviles were lords of the manor from the time of Richard I., till the year 1624, when the family became extinct. It then passed to the Berners, and in 1727 was sold to Sir Robert Brown, who was created a baronet in the fifth year of the reign of George II., and who was successively the king's resident at Venice, and paymaster of his Majesty's works; and also member of parliament for the borough of Ilchester. Sir Robert died, leaving no issue, and bequeathed the estate to his wife, Lady Brown, who was a member of the old Anglo-Irish family of Helsham, of the County of Kilkenny. From her the estate has passed through several members of this family to its present owner, who has made extensive improvements in the hall, and on the demesne generally.

LYNFORD HALL,
The Seat of MRS. LYNE STEPHENS,

Is a splendid mansion, only recently occupied. It is of Elizabethan style of architecture, and constructed of red brick and Little Castorton and Ketton stone. It was erected by the late Stephens Lyne Stephens, Esq., from the designs of Mr. William Burn, the architect; commenced in 1857 and completed in 1862. The chimney-pieces of the dining and drawing-rooms, the library, the carved doors, and much of the decorative work, were executed in Paris. Lynford Hall is distant about eight miles from Thetford.

MANNINGTON HALL,
The Seat of the Right Hon. the EARL OF ORFORD.

This manor was conveyed to the Walpole family about the year 1736, after the death of Sir Charles and Lady Potts, whose family had been settled here since the year 1270. The present Hall of Orford has considerably improved and added to the old manor-house, which now contains many portraits and pictures of great historical interest. Mannington is five miles from Aylsham.

MARHAM HOUSE,
The Seat of HENRY VILLEBOIS, ESQ.,

Situated about seven miles from Swaffham, is a neat and commodious mansion of modern construction.

MELTON CONSTABLE,
The Seat of the RIGHT HON. LORD HASTINGS.

This princely estate has been held by the Astley family for many centuries, and here was a fine old hall, said to date from the time of the Conquest, a portion of which still forms part of the offices to the present hall, which was built by Sir Jacob Astley in 1680, and to which many additions have been subsequently made. It is a noble square building, of brick and stone, with four fronts; and the chapel, grand staircase, and many of the apartments, ceilings, &c., are highly finished. In this hall are most valuable collections of articles of vertu, and antiquities. Melton Constable is situated about six and a half miles from Fakenham.

GREAT MELTON HALL,
The residence of the Rev. Henry Evans Lombe, is an ancient Elizabethan mansion, built in 1611 by one of the Anguish family; and is situated about six miles from Norwich.

MERTON HALL,

The Seat of the Right Hon. Lord Walsingham.

In the time of Edward the Confessor, this estate belonged to the Saxon chief, Alid; but at the time of the Norman Conquest it was seized by the victor, and by him bestowed upon Ralph Baynard, a companion in his invasion. The heiress of Ralph Baynard married Sir Thomas de Grey, who settled here in 1327. His descendant, Sir William de Grey, was born at Merton in 1719, and after having successively filled the offices of Solicitor-General, Attorney-General, and Lord Chief Justice of the Common Pleas, was, on October 17th, 1780, created Baron Walsingham. Merton Hall is a fine Elizabethan brick mansion, which was rebuilt in 1610, thoroughly repaired about thirty years ago, and has since been enlarged by the present Lord Walsingham. It is distant about two miles from Watton.

MIDDLETON TOWER,

The Seat of Lewis Whincop Jarvis, Esq.

The ancient and celebrated family of Scales, who founded this castle, were Lords of the Manor of Middleton at a very early period, and probably in the reign of Henry II. erected the building then known as Tyrrington Hall, of which the gate-house, shown in our view, is probably a portion. This Tower is a lofty and massive brick pile, with stone casing, seventy-two feet in height, fifty-four in length, and thirty-three in breadth. Lord Scales obtained the manor in marriage with the heiress of Jeffery de Lisewis, and the family was seated here till the reign of Edward IV., when their heiress married Earl Rivers. From whom the estate passed through various families to its present owner, who has restored and added considerably to its magnificent appearance. It is situated about four miles from Lynn, and seen from the railway station at Middleton, it has a very attractive and imposing appearance.

NARBOROUGH HALL,

The Seat of R. Marriott, Esq.

This Mansion was built by Judge Spelman, in the reign of Henry VIII. and had formerly a moat surrounding it. It was once famed for the large collection of ancient and modern coins and medals it contained, which was said to be the most valuable in Europe. It is situated about five miles from Swaffham.

NECTON HALL,

The Seat of Colonel Mason,

Is distant from Swaffham four miles. The Mason family have been settled here since 1452.

OXBURGH CASTLE,

The Seat of Sir Henry Bedingfeld, Bart.,

Is a fine specimen of the architecture of the olden time. It was built in the latter end of the 15th century by Sir Edmund Bedingfeld, who was knighted at the coronation of Richard III. in 1483, and who had the previous year obtained a grant or patent from Edward IV., dated July 3, 1482, to erect a manor-house with towers, battlements, machicolations, &c. It is built of brick, and was originally of a square form, enclosing a court 118 feet long and 92 feet broad, round which the apartments were ranged. The entrance is over a bridge (formerly a drawbridge), through an arched gateway between two turreted octagonal towers, eighty feet high. In the western tower is a winding staircase, beautifully turned, and lighted by quadrefoil eyelet-holes. The other tower is divided into four stories, each forming an octagonal room, with arched ceilings, stone window-frames, and stone fireplaces. The archway between the towers is supposed by numerous proofs, and over it is a large and handsome room, thirty-three feet long by twenty feet broad, called the "King's Room," having one window to the north, and two bay windows to the south; the floor is paved with small, fine bricks, and the walls are covered with very curious tapestry, which exhibits several figures of princes, and ladies and gentlemen, of the time of Henry VII., who is supposed to have lodged in this apartment when he visited Oxburgh. Queen Elizabeth once visited this famous hall, and lodged in the apartment over the king's room. The great banqueting-room, which stood on the south side of the quadrangle, was taken down in 1788. It was fifty-six feet long and twenty-nine feet wide, and had an arched oak roof, resembling that in Westminster Hall, and two oriel windows. The outer walls of the hall stand in the broad and deep moat, fifty-two feet in breadth, and ten feet in depth, which is well supplied from the adjacent rivulet. Oxburgh is distant three miles from Stoke Ferry.

QUIDDENHAM HALL,

The Seat of the Right Hon. the Earl of Albermarle,

About two miles from East Harling. The estate, originally belonging to William de Quiddenham, finally passed into the hands of two sisters, of the name of Holland, and was by them sold to Mr. Thinton, a merchant, who sold it, in 1702, to George, third Earl of Albermarle, the descendant of a noble Dutch family, that came over to England with William III. The house is large, and principally built of brick. The park front comprises two divisions; the two wings project with a slight curve, and the centre is thrown back, the lower part being brought parallel to the rest of the front by a stone portion, of the Doric order, surmounted with balustrades. The garden front also consists of a centre, and two wings, the centre having four Ionic columns, that support an entablature and pediment, while at the wing are two corresponding pilasters.

RACKHEATH HALL,

The Seat of Sir Henry J. Stracey, Bart.,

Is a handsome white brick mansion, in the Italian style, which has been much improved by its present owner. The house contains some fine paintings, amongst which are a Vandyck, and a very valuable Rubens, representing Coriolanus before Rome. The chief entrance to the park is through the elegant iron gates from the Great Exhibition of 1851. It is distant four and a-half miles from Norwich.

RAYNHAM HALL,

The Seat of the Most Hon. the Marquis Townshend,

Is three miles from Fakenham. The estate came into the possession of the Townshend family as early as the reign of Henry I., by the marriage of Frederic Townshend, a noble Norman, to Elizabeth, the daughter and heiress of Sir Thomas de Grevill. Sir Roger Townshend, in 1630, built the present edifice, after a plan of Inigo Jones. Charles, the second Viscount Townshend, modernised the mansion, added a wing, and altered the principal apartments. It contains a valuable and choice collection of pictures, including the far-famed Salvator Rosa, given to Charles, Lord Viscount Townshend, Secretary of State, by Frederick the Great.

SALL HALL,

The Seat of the Rev. Sir Edward Repps Jodrell, Bart.

The old hall at Sall was situated at the north-east end of the parish, and was for many generations the seat of the Repps family. The present hall was built in 1761, by Edward Hall, Esq., M.P., who married a great grandmother of the present baronet, who succeeded his father in 1801. Sall is a mile and a-half distant from Reepham.

SANDRINGHAM HALL,

The Seat of His Royal Highness the Prince of Wales.

Of this mansion we have given two views, and though many alterations and extensions will no doubt be made from time to time, to meet the requirements of the Prince's establishment, it is not probable that the general appearance of the present hall will be altered. The Sandringham estate was purchased by His Royal Highness in 1862, for the sum of £220,000, of the Hon. C. S. Cowper; and since that time, improvements thereon have been in constant progress.

TAVERHAM HALL,

The Seat of the Rev. JOHN NATHANIEL MICKLETHWAIT,

Distant five and a-half miles from Norwich, is a newly-erected Tudor mansion, built of red brick with stone dressings. The apartments are spacious and lofty, and have finely moulded ceilings. The house contains several valuable paintings.

THURSFORD HALL,

The Seat of JOSEPH J. SCOTT-CHAD, ESQ.,

Is a house of the period of Queen Elizabeth, and was built in 1689, on the site of a still older one. The elevation presents a long embattled front, broken by three large projecting bay windows, to the height of two storeys; the intervening space is also occupied by two mullioned windows. Many alterations have been made by successive owners. The porch, with its columns, pediments, and circular arch of entrance, is of a more modern character. The large piers, surmounted with balls, at the gate to the office, are probably of the same date. In the reign of Charles II. it was the residence of Thomas Guybon, Esq. In 1753 it was bought by George Chad, Esq., Recorder of Lynn, who retired here from the arduous duties of his profession. He was created a baronet in 1791. From his son, Sir Charles Chad, it passed in 1856 to his great nephew, the present owner, by whom it has recently been nearly rebuilt, and who has made large additions to and improvements in it. It is distant five miles from Fakenham.

WESTACRE HIGH HOUSE,

The Seat of ANTHONY HAMOND, ESQ.,

Is said to derive its name from the circumstance of its being situated on some of the highest ground in the county of Norfolk. It is distant six and a-half miles from Swaffham.

WESTON HOUSE,

The Seat of Lieut.-Col. HAMBLETON FRANCIS CUSTANCE,

Is situated about five miles from Reepham, and on the turnpike road from Norwich to Fakenham. The Weston estate first came into the possession of the Custance family in 1726, and the old hall, now a farm-house, which was built by their predecessors, the Richewoods (who had the estate from a very early period) and added to by an ancestor of the present owner, was partially pulled down and the present house built, under the direction of Mr. Hawkins, the architect, in 1779-80. The interior fittings are more elegant than the plainness of the exterior would lead one to expect, and the house contains several handsome rooms, in which are some valuable paintings, among others, a fine picture by West. The marble decorations were brought from Rome.

WESTWICK HOUSE,

The Seat of JOHN BERNEY PETRE, ESQ.,

Is within three miles of North Walsham, and has been considered one of the most delightfully situated seats in the county. It was erected in the reign of Queen Anne, by John Berney, Esq.

GREAT WITCHINGHAM HALL,

The Seat of HENRY KETT TOMPSON, ESQ.,

Is situated about three miles and-half south of Reepham, near Lenwade Bridge, and is a large brick mansion, with embattled towers.

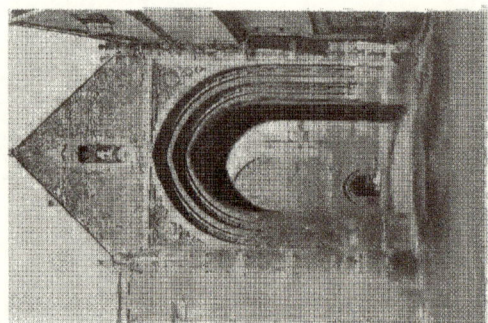

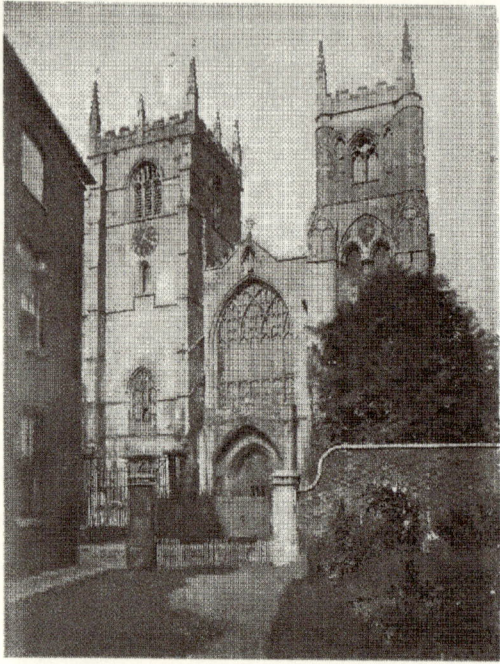

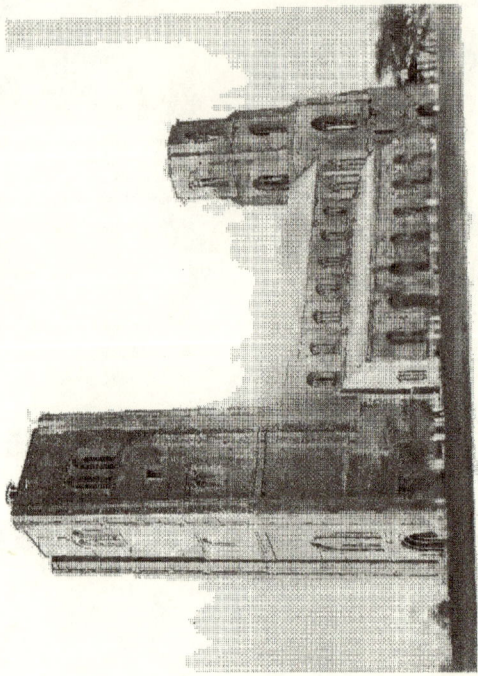

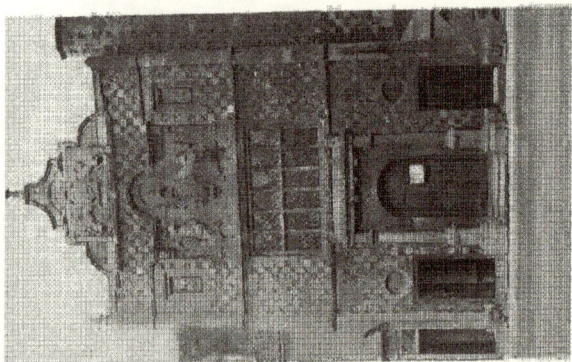

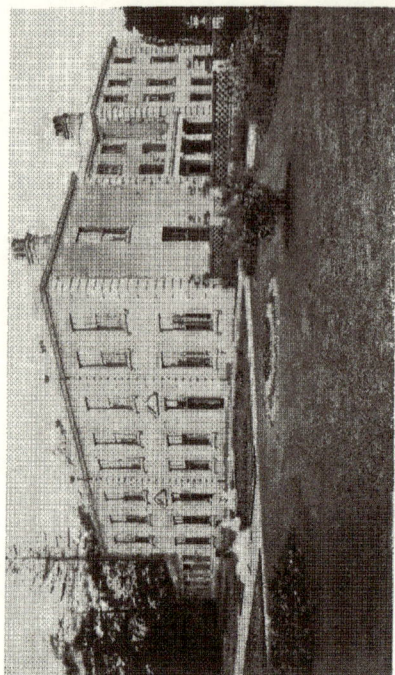

MIDDLE ST. SOME OTHER FORMING A STREET FORMING A STREET EATING A PT. OF, LONDON

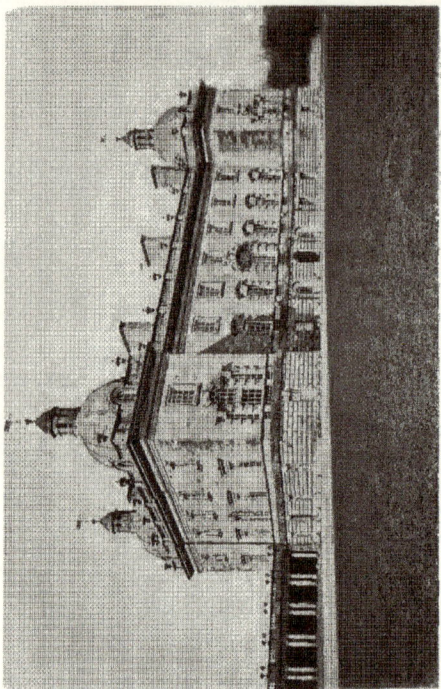

MEMBER'S LODGE

MULBROC* 38.S'UILES STREET, NORWICH * S&AIO BOMD.ST.LONDON

KIRMOND TOFTS HALL.

INGLETHORPE HALL, EAST?

YALE HALL

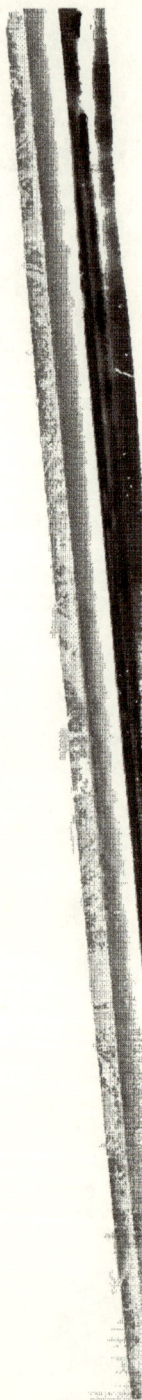

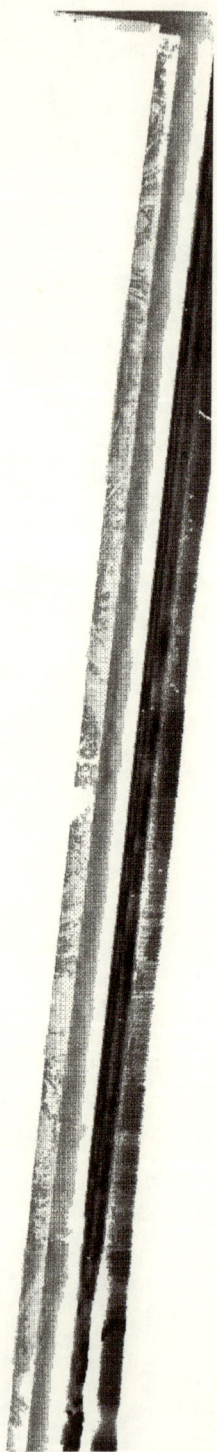

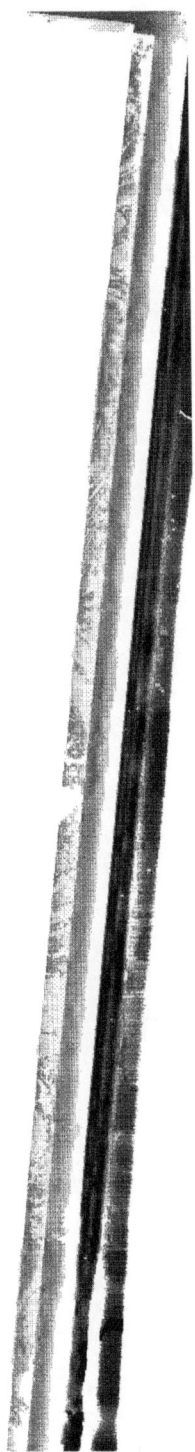

www.ingramcontent.com/pod-product-compliance
Lightning Source LLC
Chambersburg PA
CBHW030851270326
41928CB00008B/1327